**W9-BIG-959**

The Church on Earth

Ronald A. Knox

# The Church on Earth

The Nature and Authority
of the Catholic Church, and
the Place of the Pope within It

SOPHIA INSTITUTE PRESS®
Manchester, New Hampshire

Sophia Institute Press®
Box 5284, Manchester, NH 03108
1-800-888-9344
www.sophiainstitute.com

*Nihil obstat:* Thomas McLaughlin, S.T.D., *Censor deputatus*
*Imprimatur:* Edm. Can. Surmont, *Vicarius generalis*
Westminster, December 3, 1928

**Library of Congress Cataloging-in-Publication Data**

Knox, Ronald Arbuthnott, 1888-1957.
    The church on earth : the nature and authority of the
        Catholic Church, and the place of the pope within it /
        Ronald A. Knox.
        p. cm.
    ISBN 1-928832-83-0 (pbk.)
    1. Catholic Church.  I. Title.
    BX1751.3.K64 2003
    262'.02 — dc21                                    2003001372

03  04  05  06  07  08  09  10  9  8  7  6  5  4  3  2  1

# Contents

## Part Three: The seat of
## authority in the Church

The Church on Earth

Part One

# The nature
# of the Church

Chapter One

# The Church is
# a visible society

The Catholic Church defines herself as a visible society. The appropriateness of the term is not immediately obvious. It might be objected, for example, that all societies are visible insofar as their members can be seen — so many individuals of the human species — and that no society could be visible in any other sense. The meaning of the phrase is made clearer if we say that the Church is visibly a society; that it is a body which acts corporately and that its capacity for doing so is manifested by the effect of those actions upon history.

But perhaps the simplest way of elucidating this point is to take instances from ordinary life. It would be perfectly intelligible to talk of all the Old Etonians in the world as constituting a single society. The number of them is exactly defined: you are an Old Etonian, or you are not. Old Etonians are all bound together, however vaguely, by common memories, a common tradition, and common loyalties. But they do not constitute a visible society; they have no principle of cohesion that enables them to act as a single body, nor have they any mutual relations with one another — only a common relation to their old school. But a body exists, known as the Old Etonian Association, which is a visible society. Its members, besides being alumni of the same school, form a corporate body; they have common rules, common rights, and a common principle of cohesion (in this case, an elected committee). The association can act as a body, can hold property under a legal title, and so on. "Old Etonians" is a name that describes merely a collection of persons. "The Old Etonian Association" describes a body of persons.

The Protestant theory of the Church, when Protestantism had a coherent theology, represented the Church as merely a collection of people. Individual bodies there might be — the Presbyterians, the Brownists, the Baptists, and so on — each of which had a legal corporate existence. But "the Church" was neither any one of these nor the whole conglomeration of these; it was simply the total muster, known only to God, of those names which were inscribed in the Book of Life. There was no question of salvation in or through the Church; you were a member of the Church precisely because you were being saved.

Membership in such a Church involved no mutual relations, but only a common personal relation to our Lord Jesus Christ. Members of any sect, however strict, who were not actually predestined to eternal life were not to be regarded as members of the Church in any sense at all. Conversely, those who were predestined to eternal life could attain it without membership (even "in desire") of any visible society whatsoever.

Catholic theology, in contrast to all this, represents membership (at least "in desire"[1]) of a visible Church as the indispensable means to salvation; man finds himself, for supernatural purposes, not as a lonely unit, but as a member of a body corporate. The Church, then, in Catholic theory, is a visible society; like other visible societies, it will have its rights, its duties, its ascertainable figures of membership, and its center of cohesion. Its members will be in mutual relation, partly by means of a common life and partly by means of subordination. The Church will,

---

[1] "Every man who is ignorant of the Gospel of Christ and of His Church, but seeks the truth and does the will of God in accordance with his understanding of it, can be saved. It may be supposed that such persons would have desired Baptism explicitly if they had known its necessity" (*Catechism of the Catholic Church*, par. 1260).

moreover, act as a whole; it will have its defined interactions with the world outside it. It will be a body, not a mere group.

Infinitely the most important among these relations is its corporate relation to the Person of our Lord Jesus Christ. But in these pages, our attention will be confined to the Church on earth — to its organization considered as one of the many organizations under which, in our present experience, our fellowmen are grouped.

It must be remembered, however, that this division of the subject is adopted only for the purpose of systematic arrangement. It is not to be supposed that there are two Churches of Christ: one an external, workaday fact, with laws, constitutions, etc., and the other a supernatural entity, Christ's glorious Bride, an ideal society in Heaven. There is but one Church, seen in Heaven as the totality of humankind redeemed, seen on earth as an organization that struggles, suffers, has enemies, and — so far as its members, even the highest of them, are human — has faults.

When Aristotle said that "man is a political animal," he did not mean that man has a natural craving for registering votes, for frequenting assemblies, and for making public speeches. He meant that man is by nature "club-able" — that it is his instinct to form groups, not (like the animals) for merely practical purposes, but as the condition of realizing himself. Just as the institutions of Christianity — prayer, worship, sacraments, sacrifice, etc. — have their dim analogue in the religions that man, fallen and unilluminated, invents for himself, so the Catholic Church itself is the full satisfaction of that instinct for solidarity which inspires man even in his primitive state.

If our Lord Jesus Christ had merely left behind Him a school of philosophy, whose influence was to leaven the mass of human thought, He would not have provided an outlet for that sentiment of loyalty toward the group which is characteristic of the human genius. The instinct that bade the three hundred Spartans at Thermopylae to fight to the last, in obedience to the holy laws of their country, the instinct that encouraged Japanese subjects to commit suicide by way of celebrating an event in the life of the royal family, would have in that case no echo and no analogy in the perfect world-system.

Almighty God, who disposes the natural and the supernatural orders in correspondence with each other, did not see fit to leave His new creation warped and one-sided. The religion He revealed to us was from the first indissolubly associated with the formation of a new religious group, which was to have higher claims upon our loyalty than country, party, and even the family itself.

Yet the Church, like the other institutions of Christianity, was foreshadowed under the old Jewish dispensation, lest the world should be unprepared for it. The word itself is borrowed from the terminology of the Hebrew religion. The *Ecclesia* or Assembly of God was, under the old covenant, conterminous with a single nation, the people of the Jews. Patriotism itself, for this one people, was transmuted into a higher obligation by the unique relation in which that people stood to the one true God. This one people had been "called out" among all the nations of the earth; as God Himself was unique, it was His unique assembly. It was as a participant in the rights of that assembly that the Jew claimed what he claimed, hoped what he hoped; his citizenship was his churchmanship. And it was this Church-nation that served, in God's providence, as the rough model for the Christian assembly that followed and superseded it.

The organization to which our Lord sometimes referred as "my Church," but more often as "the kingdom of God" or "the kingdom of Heaven," was to differ in many ways from the old "Church of God," which had been led by Moses through the wilderness. It was to differ from it in being international; it was to differ from it in being guided and indwelt by the Holy Spirit; and it was to differ from it in being indefectible and irreplaceable.

But plainly the new Church was to be, like the old "Church," a visible society, for in all His teaching, our Lord uttered no hint of a difference that must have proved so momentous. Nay, He was at pains more than once to emphasize the visible character of the Church He came to found. An invisible Church, by its very definition, would number no adherents who were not ultimately destined to eternal life.

But our Lord's Church does contain unworthy members, the cockle among the wheat, the worthless fish in the net, the man who came in without a wedding garment.[2] It is not only of the old Church but of the new that He warns us repeatedly, "Many are called (*kletoi*, members of the *ekklesia*), but few are chosen."[3] An assembly of human souls so diverse in their destiny must have, clearly, a visible, external structure; must have a principle of membership in which grace indeed plays a part, but not, directly, the grace of predestination.

[2] Matt. 13:24-30, 36-43, 47-49; 22:11-14.
[3] Matt. 22:14.

# The Church on Earth

We could infer, then, from our Lord's own words what we learn from Catholic theology: that the Church on earth is a visible institution among other visible institutions. Judas Iscariot proved to be a rotten member of it, but he was a member of it for all that. In aspiration, it is the society of the elect, but in fact, here and now, it is the society of those who have been redeemed by the Precious Blood, whether that redemption will finally have its salutary effect or not.

Chapter Two

# The Church is supernatural

The Church, then, is not some ideal entity. It is a visible, working society among the other visible, working societies under which humanity is organized. At the same time, it differs entirely in one essential point from all the others: it is a supernatural society.

There are numerous bodies that encourage and help their members to attain a supernatural end. The Quakers, for example, are attempting, according to their lights, to attain a supernatural end, and the Society of Friends, by the standard that it sets before them and by the sympathetic cooperation of their fellow members, doubtless helps them to do so. Exactly the same is true of certain bodies that call themselves "churches" — for example, the Church of England.

But the Catholic Church claims something more than this. She claims that membership in her own body, at least "in desire," is essential to the attainment of a supernatural end, is a necessary means of human salvation. And that means that the Church is herself supernatural. The stream does not rise higher than its source, nor could we Christians think of ourselves as being regenerated in the womb of the Church if she herself were not endued with life-giving power.

Every other "body" in the world is, in the last resort, only the sum of its members; they get out of it what they put into it, and no more. But the Catholic Church is not simply ourselves (although she is ourselves); she is also our Mother. It is we who depend on her, not she on us, for spiritual existence. In her are stored up, as in a reservoir, the graces that manifest themselves in her children. As the body that makes other things manifest must itself be light, so the Body that supernaturalizes us must itself be supernatural.

Chapter Three

# The Church is faultless

We said that the Church, so far as her members, even the highest of them, are human, has faults. This qualification is an important one. For the Church, as such, is a faultless society.

It is difficult to conceive any proposition that would call forth more indignant protests from non-Catholics and more demands for explanation from Catholics themselves. Surely, however great our loyalty to the Church may be, we have to admit that there have been times when bishops used the authority that had been entrusted to them to propagate error or to subserve the purposes of tyranny; nay, that popes themselves, especially in the days when they had all the responsibilities attached to a territorial sovereignty, have perverted justice, followed temporal ends, and given occasion to the enemies of the Christian religion to blaspheme.

How can all this be true, if the Church is a faultless society?

# The Church on Earth

Yet it is evident that, in our view, the Church must be faultless. Protestant bodies are always eager to confess the "failure" of "the Church" or "the churches," precisely because at the back of their minds, they think of churches as manmade institutions, as voluntary associations that reflect, in an intensified degree, the failings of the human beings who have formed and compose them. With this thought at the back of their minds, it is only natural — it is only the part of modesty — that they should confess failure as an imperfection; more, that they should ask themselves, as they often do ask themselves, whether the fault lies partly in the nature of organizations to which they belong; whether there is something inherently wrong in the system that can produce such barren results.

This is not the language of Catholics, nor the process of their thought. There have been times when, locally, the prospects of any revival in the direction of Catholicism have seemed infinitely remote — in England, for example, during the second half of the eighteenth century. At such times, Catholics do well to accuse themselves of insufficient zeal; they will be tempted to doubt, sometimes, the wisdom of those who rule them. But they will not say that the Church has failed, for that would seem to imply that the religious system to which they are attached is capable of change and of improvement. They do not think of the Catholic Church as an imperfect, uncertain instrument for preserving and propagating the Catholic Faith. The Catholic Church, like the Catholic Faith, is to them an end in itself, something intrinsically desirable, which they are bound to maintain at all costs. It is not the Church that fails; it is her representatives.

The reason for this confidence is not far to seek. Catholics believe that their Church is directly of divine institution. It is not a system that men, after earnest prayer and thoughtful deliberation, have devised as the best scheme that they could think of for perpetuating the work of their Master, Christ. It is directly God's handiwork — no less directly than this visible creation in which we find ourselves. Just as in creation there is nothing, strictly speaking, imperfect, i.e., nothing that fails to conduce to its proper end, unless it is owing to the fall of guilty man, so in the Church there can be nothing imperfect except what is due to the individual failings of her members. We can no more doubt that we live in the best of all possible churches than that we live in the best of all possible worlds.

When the representatives of non-Catholic bodies gather to discuss problems of reunion, one of the subjects most frequently raised is the question whether episcopal government belongs to the *esse* or to the *bene esse* of the Church, whether it does or does not form an essential feature in the "witness" of the bodies that are organized on that system. It would be impossible for Catholics to treat such questions as open to discussion; the episcopacy, and for that matter the papacy, must be regarded, not as part of the witness that the Catholic Church bears, but as part of herself. She could no more think of herself without them than she could propose to repeal a law of nature. That is what she is like, for better or worse; and because she believes in the goodness of God, she believes that he has constituted His Church in the best possible way.

Ideally, the perfection of the Church lies in the perfection of her members. It is in virtue of the graces individually bestowed upon them that she will be ultimately manifested as the Bride of Christ, "not having spot or wrinkle or any such thing."[4] Meanwhile, she is a faultless society in the sense that her organization is perfectly designed to lead her members to perfection if they will. To preserve the unity of the Faith, to remain in Catholic obedience, may be only a very short step on the road toward

[4] Eph. 5:27.

perfection, but it is the first, indispensable step. This is the soil in which the flowers of sanctity are meant to blossom. To be a Christian is not only to live a Christian life, not only to hold a Christian theology, but to belong to a Christian assembly.

Chapter Four

# The Church is permanent

When Almighty God made a covenant with His ancient people, the Jews, He fortified it with promises that made the Jews generally suppose that it was eternal and unalterable. They supposed that, whatever changes affected human fortunes, it would be the Jewish race and the Jewish race alone that would always stand out among the nations as the chosen people of God. This point of view, all Christians would admit, was a mistaken one.

Almighty God did — so Christians hold — replace His old national *Ecclesia* by a new *Ecclesia* that was to be international and unpolitical. How, then, can we be certain that this new *Ecclesia* is permanent, any more than the old? If God has reshaped His plans once, why should He not reshape them again? Why should not a still newer dispensation be substituted for the Catholic Church, as the Catholic Church was substituted for the Judaism that preceded it?

# The Church on Earth

There have indeed been heretical thinkers, in the Middle Ages especially, who did not shrink from such an affirmation. With a plausible appearance of symmetry, they suggested that each Person of the Blessed Trinity in turn was to regulate the world-order. The Old Dispensation had been the dispensation of God the Father. The Catholic Church was the dispensation of God the Son. Now, they said, a third world-order was to begin, which was to be the dispensation of the Holy Spirit. Again and again, such notions have been made the basis for new, "enthusiastic" movements among Christian people, even down to our own day. The Irvingites, with their new set of Apostles who were destined to leave a survivor at the Last Judgment, were perhaps the most recent in public memory.

All such systems of thought imply that the Catholic Church fulfilled for a time the purpose for which God ordained it, albeit temporarily, albeit inadequately; but that it can be, now or at some later date, superseded. Thus it was fashionable among heretics in the Middle Ages to claim that the Catholic Church committed suicide in accepting the alleged "Donation of Constantine," and changing from a spiritual into a political body.

It is obvious, upon a little reflection, that the analogy is misleading. For, if we take the promises made to the

Jews as a complete body of prophecy, we shall find constant allusions to the advent of a Messiah who will deliver, not the whole Jewish people, but a remnant of it, who will set up a kingdom of peace and of justice, and so on. The Old Covenant, then, was expressly and admittedly a temporary expedient; it looked forward to and waited for a fuller revelation in the Messiah who was to come. Moses foretold a prophet greater than himself. David sang of a King, his own more glorious posterity.

But this new kingdom was hailed, from the first, as a permanent world-order — an everlasting kingdom (so it was revealed to Daniel[5]) which should not be destroyed. And accordingly our Lord Himself proclaimed that His kingdom was a final and an irreplaceable revelation. The gates of Hell should not prevail against His Church; He would be with His Apostles all days, even to the consummation of the world.[6] And in His parables, He constantly distinguishes between two divine moments: that at which His Church is founded (the field planted, the net cast, the King setting out on a long journey, etc.) and that at which the world itself is to come to an end (the field reaped, the

[5] Cf. Dan. 2:44.
[6] Matt. 16:18; 28:20.

31

net drawn in, the King's return). It is from her own Master that the Church has learned to recognize herself as a permanent institution, which will be found still doing God's work when He comes again in judgment.

Theoretically, this condition would be realized even if, at the Last Judgment, the Church had dwindled to a mere handful of Christians, still maintaining a hierarchy and a Sovereign Pontiff. But it is the common belief of Catholics that the Church will always be recognizable as individually the most numerous among the Christian bodies. Otherwise it would be difficult for men to detect in her that note of catholicity which is distinctive of her.

Once again, the Catholic attitude on this point differs sharply from that which you will come across, in all probability, if you discuss such subjects with any representative of the reformed churches. Such men will commonly tell you that they do not expect those who come after them to be bound, necessarily, by the same traditions as they themselves are. The Church of the future, they will tell you, will probably be an institution different from any existing institution. Some hold that it will be a vast amalgamation of Protestant bodies, which will have at last settled their differences or agreed to ignore them. Others will suggest that the future lies with a reformed

"Catholicism," only to be achieved when Rome is purged of her "errors" and abandons the exclusive attitude that at present makes reunion with her impossible. Scarcely anyone supposes that, two or three hundred years hence, his own religious body will remain what it is today, upholding the same distinctive traditions that mark it out from the other Christianities.

Catholics alone, because they believe their Church to be a faultless society, and its organization a direct expression of God's will, are confident in the belief that their great-grandchildren will profess exactly the same religion as they themselves.

Chapter Five

# The Church is one

We can describe the Catholic Church as the one Church, or we can say the Catholic Church is one. The meaning of the word *one* is different in the two cases. We describe the Catholic Church as "the one Church," meaning that any body of Christians out of communion with her cannot properly be described as a church. We say the Catholic Church is one, meaning that there are no divisions within her that mar her unity. In fact, the oneness of the Church means in the first place that she is wholly unique, and in the second place that she is wholly unified.

Yet the two statements are, in effect, a denial of the same error. It matters little whether we define the attitude of Protestants by saying that they believe in a Church that is divided, or by saying that they believe in a plurality of churches. The whole issue depends upon your answer to the question, "What happens when there is a schism in the Christian body? What is left?" If you answer, "Two churches" or "Two divided parts of the Church," you are not a Catholic. If you say, "One Church and one sect," you are in agreement with Catholic Christendom.

It is no part of our present business to prove (as can be very clearly proved either from Scripture or from common sense) that the Catholic belief on this subject is the true one. This is a manual, not of apologetics, but of doctrine; it is sufficient, therefore, to consider what Catholics mean by this claim without entering into their justification for asserting it.

It might be urged — indeed, I cannot conceive why it is not urged more frequently — that the Protestant idea of Christendom differs from the Catholic idea precisely as the modern British conception of empire differs from the ancient Roman conception of it.

It might be argued that Catholic ideas on the subject date back to the association of the Church with the Roman empire in its later phases. At that time, the gradual extension of Roman citizenship almost over the whole of the known world had produced, indeed, a far more efficient type of government, yet at a cost — for the rest of the world had lost its individuality in an attempt to ape the manners and the ideas of Rome. Is it not precisely the same charge that is constantly brought against Catholicism — that it obliterates or tends to obliterate national individuality by imposing everywhere a uniform and, at bottom, a Roman culture? Whereas the British Empire aims at being, and partly is, an association of self-governing commonwealths under an attachment, hardly more than ideal, to the Crown of England. Why should not the Protestants similarly think of Christendom as a vast empire, in which each religious denomination manages its own affairs, yet all are united under the supreme headship of our Lord Jesus Christ?

To state the case so would be to state it wrongly. The difference is not a mere difference of ideals, one side declaring for a uniform standard of religion and the other for the recognition of local peculiarities. The difference is that the Catholic Church has a real principle of cohesion. The Protestant bodies are not, as a matter of fact, federated; the best witness of that is that they are constantly deploring the absence of any such federation, and holding conferences to discuss the distant possibility of achieving it. It may at some future time be achieved; Protestant Christendom may conceivably become a visible society. But it would still be in a totally different position from Catholic Christendom, because its federation would be voluntary and artificial; it might (and in all probability would) break up again within the course of a hundred years, whereas the unity of the Catholic Church cannot be broken up; its principle of cohesion is internal to itself, and defections from it, however numerous, would still leave it an integral whole.

The Church, in the Catholic view, is essentially one and essentially unique. No circumstances could arise in which there could be two true churches, or two parts of the true Church, out of visible communion with one another. This principle would hold, even if the separation of the two bodies was entirely without reference to doctrinal matters; there can be schism without heresy.

Indeed, in the days of the anti-popes, there were two separate bodies of Christians, each holding the same identical doctrines and each claiming to be in communion with the lawfully elected Pope. Were there not then, it may be asked, two Catholic Churches? Or at least two separated parts of the Catholic Church? There were not. There was, at any given moment, one Pope who was in fact lawfully elected, and those who defied his excommunication were, *de facto*, in a state of schism. The schism in question was only a material, not a formal, sin, because in the tangled state of the question, a man could do no better than follow the best light he had; and, indeed, there were men whom the Catholic Church recognizes as saints who were in fact schismatic, although their schism was inculpable. Such men (for they were Catholics) did not imagine that there were two true Churches of Christ. They did their best to discover which was the true Church, and if they failed, it was by an error for which they cannot be held responsible.

Such considerations, confusing as they may appear, arise naturally out of the reflection that the Church is directly the institution of Almighty God. He is One, and His Truth is One, and the Body that He has commissioned to teach us that Truth is one Body. The guidance that is guaranteed to us is guaranteed to a single body, and if there were more than one body in existence that could legitimately contest the title, all our certainty about revelation would perish in that moment. Any voluntary association of Christians that, under the name of a church, holds out for men's acceptance a series of religious articles agreed upon after earnest prayer and discussion, may well feel a scruple about "unchurching" another voluntary association that differs from it in detail. But such hesitations would be impossible for a society that was ordained by Almighty God to be the pillar and ground of truth.

41

Chapter Six

# The Church is hierarchical

The primary purpose of a religious organization is the offering of common worship to God. So essentially is this the business of the Church that the word *Ecclesia* is used in the New Testament to denote the gathering of Christians for worship, and the building in which this gathering takes place is called, in all languages and by almost all religious denominations, a church. Each congregation is, as it were, the Universal Church in miniature. In most religious bodies, some kind of ministry exists; men are set apart to lead the congregation in prayer, to expound religious ideas, and to perform certain ceremonies. The Catholic Church has sacramental rites, and most of these can and may be performed only by duly ordained ministers.

It would not be in place here to consider the theory of sacraments or the theory of ordination in general. What concerns us here is to examine more closely the phrase just used: "can and may be performed."

There is a distinction between the *can* and the *may*. Let us restrict ourselves for purposes of convenience to the two sacraments that are of frequent repetition. Any priest who is validly ordained can say Mass validly, but in certain circumstances, he may not. And, still more important, there are only certain circumstances in which he may, and therefore can, give absolution.

To say Mass is the function for which, primarily, a priest is ordained; given the proper opportunity, he may do so unless he has specially been forbidden to do so. And further, even if he has been forbidden to do so and defies the prohibition, he can say Mass; that is, his Consecration is a perfectly valid one. But this principle does not hold for the sacrament of Confession, unless the penitent is at the point of death, in which case it is presumed that the Church "supplies" the necessary authority. In normal circumstances, a priest may not give absolution unless he has "faculties" to do so; unless, that is to say, he does so with the express authority of the bishop. And in this case, if he may not, he cannot. For absolution is a judicial act, and no judicial act can be validly performed without jurisdiction.

The sacrament of Confession is the only one in which the ministrant, normally, sits down. To sit is an expression of authority. (So we speak of our Lord as "seated" at the right hand of the Father.) The essence of his business is to judge; and a man is not competent to judge, however much learning or prudence he possesses, unless he has been commissioned to try the case, unless he has been told to act in this way. If the judge has no commission, the award is invalid. If the priest has no jurisdiction, the sins of the penitent are not remitted.

This, then, is the simplest and most obvious way in which the layman comes into contact with the authority of the Church. He confesses his sins to a priest, and the priest gives him absolution in virtue of the authority that is delegated to him by his bishop. The authority in question is not, of course, limited to the confessional. It is the bishop who commissions a priest to preach and to instruct; it is the bishop who assigns to him a special sphere, giving him duties toward and responsibility for a particular group of human souls. But it is in the sacrament of Confession that we meet the need for such authority in its most naked form.

Even if the Christian religion had been revealed in such full detail that no possible controversy could ever arise over its doctrines, that no possible need could even be felt for fresh legislation or for determining the principles upon which that legislation was to be applied in given instances, there would still be jurisdiction in the Catholic Church. There would still have to be the kind of jurisdiction that defines the position of individuals as subject to the authority, in spiritual matters, of this pastor or that.

The Catholic priest, in fact, justifies his position by a double title. He derives from the Church, not only his priestly powers, but also his mission. Since our Lord said to His Apostles "As the Father hath sent me, so also I send you,"[7] there has been no moment at which the Church has not been sending out her representatives, her ambassadors, with fixed powers over a delimited sphere of human souls.

The officials of Protestant religious bodies are for the most part content to have a vocation from God; the idea of mission is seldom emphasized, and still more seldom is the important question pressed: "Whence, ultimately, do I derive this mission to souls? Does it come to me by direct tradition from the Apostles, or do the superiors from whom it comes to me owe their own position to state interference or human contrivance?" A bishop, in spite of valid consecration, does not become *ipso facto* capable of

[7] John 20:21.

conferring mission upon priests. He can ordain them validly, but he cannot give them the right to go out and exercise their ministry unless he himself belongs to the Catholic communion and has, within that communion, an assigned sphere of authority. He cannot send unless he himself has been sent by the Universal Church.

Thus, no one who understands Catholic theology could consent for a moment to minister, however valid his ordination, to souls which had not been committed to his charge by a bishop in communion with the Holy See. But even if he should presume to do so, in one most important particular, his ministry would be not only irregular but nugatory. Lacking mission, he would be defying Catholic order; lacking jurisdiction, he would be pronouncing unavailing words of absolution over sins unremitted in Heaven.

The Church, then, involves a hierarchy, not merely in the sense that one functionary is superior to another in dignity, but in the sense that each functionary derives from a superior his commission to act in the Church's name. Without that commission, all other qualifications would be useless.

Part Two

# The authority
# of the Church

Chapter Seven

# The Church's authority
# comes from God

In dealing with the Church's hierarchical organization, the foregoing section has already familiarized us with the idea of authority. Wherever the Catholic Church exists, subordination exists; one soul has spiritual dealings with another in virtue of a commission delegated to it from a superior. In spiritual matters, the layman obeys his parish priest, that priest obeys his bishop, and that bishop, although the powers that he holds are personally his, is limited in the exercise of them by his responsibility to a higher control, that of the Holy See.

If nothing ever happened, if the Church could go along, century after century, with no controversies, no new situations to deal with, no conflict between rival interests and rival traditions, the exercise of authority would stop here; it would be a personal matter, involving no need of debates, of conclaves, or of tribunals.

But, in fact, this exercise of authority is insufficient. New fashions of thought grow up in the world and have their repercussion in theology; new departures in spiritual activity call for regulation and for adjustment; contumacious disregard of warnings from above calls for the repression of error and of misdoing. Sometimes the Church must define more clearly the content of the message that she preaches. Sometimes she must enact laws for the general well-being of her subjects. Sometimes she must decide the rights and wrongs of a charge brought by one member or group of members against another. Sometimes she must take steps to see that her decision is properly enforced. Her rulers, like other rulers, must have legislative, judicial, and coercive powers; moreover, as a teacher, she must be the living interpreter of her own teaching.

Every exercise of authority is irksome to man's natural appetite for freedom; and it is no matter of surprise if the Church, when she exercises authority, should be met with opposition, more or less determined, from the party whose interests suffer, or are likely to suffer, from her decision. It is no matter of surprise if critics from without, more distinguished for kindliness of feeling than for the capacity to mind their own business, should exclaim against her tyrannical methods or her pedantic insistence upon uniformity.

All societies do, as a matter of fact, exercise authority over their own members; most of them do so, not by direct corporate action, but by the decision of some competent authority. The principal reason why the Church, today especially, has to labor under the imputation of tyranny is that she cannot, by the very terms of her commission, become a democratic institution. The point is, not that she is a monarchy, but that she is a hierarchy. In her constitution, man receives powers delegated to him, not from man, but from God. The deference that is due to her various commands may differ in its degree; but the foundation of it is in every case the same. We obey the Church, not as we obey the rules of a voluntary association, but as we obey the voice of God.

Chapter Eight

# The Church has
# authority to teach

The authority of the Church as a teacher, and her authority as a ruler are, we must observe from the outset, two different conceptions. When we speak of an official as having authority, we mean that he holds a warrant or commission issued by some higher power. When we speak of a writer or teacher as having authority, or as being an authority, we mean that he has knowledge (or powers of judgment) superior to our own.

So, if we were to speak of acting in a particular way "on the authority of the Church," we would mean that we acted in that way because the Church told us to, or at least allowed us to. But when we speak of "believing a thing on the authority of the Church," we do not mean that we believe it because the Church allows us to or because the Church tells us to. We mean that we believe it because the Church assures us that the thing is so. The authority here is not that of a superior who empowers you to act, but that of a person with superior knowledge, whose word you are prepared to take for a piece of information. It is by appealing to authority that a policeman arrests you in the name of the King. It is by appealing to authority that a historian assumes the truth of a statement that he has found in Caesar's *Commentaries*. In either case, there is the idea of appealing to something behind you to back you up. But in the former case, your appeal is to a superior right; in the latter, it is an appeal to superior knowledge.

It is possible to have a religion without a revelation. It is possible, if you can rid yourself of the materialist prejudice, to arrive at the notion of a Creator from the evidence found in His creation. But most religions that have been operative in history have been religions depending upon some alleged revelation, the Christian religion among them. The Christian revelation was not enshrined in a book; it was enshrined in a Life. And the record of that Life was not, at first, committed to paper; there were no Gospels when the Christian message was first preached. The safeguarding of revelation depended, therefore, upon a set of firsthand witnesses who were called Apostles, and next to them upon "the elders," whose memory would go furthest back.

The Church was thus a teaching Church in its earliest beginnings. Religious certitude was based upon a set of living memories, and those memories were perpetuated in the first instance by Tradition. When St. Paul exclaims, "Though an angel from Heaven should deliver to you any other doctrine than that which you have received, let him be accursed,"[8] he shows clearly enough the attitude of primitive Christianity. The Church contained an inner core of "witnesses," whose duty it was to pass on to the world supernatural doctrines, to be accepted immediately on their authority, remotely on the authority of Jesus Christ.

It was but natural that as time went on, some of the Apostles and some of those who had listened to the Apostles should put facts and doctrines on record by writing. It was almost equally to be expected that other writings of early Christians, often fantastic and sometimes heretical in tendency, should falsely gain the reputation of apostolic authorship. Thus, a literature grew up, with varying degrees of authority corresponding to its varying degrees of authenticity. Who was to decide which of these writings were genuine and which spurious? Necessarily the Tradition of the Church was the arbiter. Thus, in time, when the heat of local partisanship had cooled, the

[8] Gal. 1:8.

Universal Church recognized certain writings as unquestionably genuine, and it is these that go to form the body of literature known as the New Testament.

It is not true to say that the New Testament depends upon the Church for its authority. The Church teaches that the Scriptures, whether of the Old or the New Testament, were written under the inspiration of the Holy Spirit and are consequently free from error; no other title is needed to claim for them the assent of Christians. Their authority springs from their own origin. But it is true to say that we would not be conscious of this authority if the Church did not assure us of its existence. In the order of our knowledge, belief in the Church is antecedent to belief in the Scriptures, and is the condition of it. Historical criticism assures us, indeed, that the books of the New Testament are veracious in their main outline, but only revelation could make us confident in the belief that they have God as their author. It is the Church that assures us, for example, that the letter of St. Jude has a higher authority than that of the letter attributed to St. Barnabas; it is the Church, further, that assures us that St. Jude wrote under the direct inspiration of the Holy Spirit.

Whatever is found clearly asserted in the Scriptures of either Testament is part of the Christian revelation. We believe it, even apart from anything that the Church may have said in affirmation or in explanation of it. We distinguish it from the doctrines actually defined by the Church as being the object of "divine" (not of "divine-Catholic") faith. To deny such an assertion is, of course, impossible for a faithful Catholic. It is not, however, heresy strictly so-called, for heresy strictly so-called is contrary to "Catholic" faith. Such belief is only an indirect attack upon the teaching authority of the Church.

It would have been possible for Almighty God to have given us a revelation in the Scriptures so complete and so unmistakable that the teaching office of the Church would have been unnecessary — or rather, that the Church would have been able to confine herself to asserting the authenticity and veracity of Scripture without further comment. But it is a commonplace of experience and of history that the Bible gives rise to various interpretations even among those who, in general, admit its veracity. It is, therefore, the office of the Church, not only to preserve the text of Scripture, but to expound it — to compare a multitude of statements, made in a variety of different contexts, and to extract from these the essential principles of theology.

It is evident that for this purpose, the Church must teach with authority. She must be able to say to a scholar, however profound his learning, "No, you have understood this passage in the wrong way. You have attached too much weight to this piece of evidence, as opposed to that. With all your learning, you are wrong." Unless some such authority exists, it is inevitable in the nature of the case that disputes should arise about interpretation such as may confuse the minds of the faithful. It is inevitable, also, in view of the temptations to cleverness that always beset the scholar's mind, that such indiscriminate interpretation will eat away, in time, the supernatural fabric of Christian doctrine, unless there is some authoritative voice to silence argument.

It might easily be supposed that if the Church is thus occupied in guaranteeing and interpreting revelation, the Church no less than the Bible must be inspired — that the same Spirit who communicated revelation to the sacred writers must have communicated it equally to the Fathers of the councils. This is altogether a misconception. The Church has not, and does not profess to have, any sort of access to fresh information about the unseen world beyond what is already contained in the deposit of Faith. This deposit includes all those beliefs which, whether explicitly asserted in Scripture or not, have been handed down to us from the earliest generation of Christians.

In what, then, does the teaching authority of the Church consist? Does she simply hand on, by means of the same unvarying formulas, the same body of doctrines that she preached in the first century? She hands on the same body of doctrines, but not necessarily in the same formulas. She is in the position of a trustee who is called upon, not merely to carry out his commission, but to interpret, from time to time, the terms of it. If two parties in any other religious denomination dispute with one another as to which represents the genuine tradition, it is sometimes necessary for them to have their differences settled by the award of a secular tribunal, like any other question of trusteeship. The Catholic Church does not appeal to such awards; she contains within herself a principle of authority divinely appointed to adjudge all possible quarrels.

Suppose that, today, some violent controversy should arise about a point of doctrine that has never hitherto been accurately defined by the Church — such a doctrine, for example, as that of the essence of the Sacrifice in the Mass, which is explained in different ways by different schools. Suppose that two strong rival bodies of theological opinion should build themselves up over this question.

Such a controversy may be settled in one of two ways: either by summoning a general council, whose members will bear testimony to the tradition that has been handed down in the several parts of the Catholic world, or by a decision made at Rome with the Supreme Pontiff's authority — which authority itself reflects the tradition handed down by the Church in Rome, the "Mother and Mistress of all Churches." In such a case, the competent authority may decide that no sufficient data exist, whether derived from documents or from oral tradition, for pronouncing judgment. If so, the two rival views will still be equally tenable; and sometimes (as in the famous controversy over grace) the competent authority will forbid either side, under pain of sin, to attach the stigma of heresy to the rival view. Or a definite decision may be given in favor of one party.

If such a decision is given, the teaching that it enshrines becomes, thenceforth, part of the official teaching of the Catholic Church. The contrary teaching, thenceforth, will be formal heresy. The stigma of heresy will not attach to the name of any theologian who has taught such contrary doctrine during nineteen hundred years of Christendom; it will be recognized that such theologians, writing when they did, had a right to their liberty of opinion, since they failed to see that their teaching was not in accordance with Christian Tradition. In future, however, anyone who embraces their opinions will be *ipso facto* guilty of heresy.

In acting thus, the Church has not added anything to the body of her doctrines. No positive element has entered into her theology that was not there before; she has only clarified her doctrine by discarding what was, she says, an inadequate interpretation of them all the time. As a rule, indeed, this clarification will involve the use of a terminology hitherto not used, or not universally used. She could not, for example, safeguard her theology against misrepresentations of St. Paul's teaching about the Incarnation without using words such as *Person* and *nature*, which are not part of St. Paul's own theological vocabulary. She could not vindicate against sophistical interpretation the vivid faith of, say, St. John Chrysostom,[9] about the Blessed Sacrament, without using a distinction between "substance" and "accidents" with which St. John Chrysostom would have been unfamiliar in such a context. She could not say what St. Leo[10] would have said

---

[9] St. John Chrysostom (c. 347-407), Archbishop of Constantinople and Doctor; named Chrysostom, or "Golden Mouth" for his eloquent preaching.

[10] St. Leo the Great (d. 461), Pope from 440 and Doctor.

(had he been alive) in condemnation of Gallicanism without using un-Leonine terms such as *irreformable*. She acts, on such occasions, not as legislator, but as judge; and it is the judge's business to interpret law, not to make it.

In all this, the Church as such has no divine guarantee of inspiration. Doubtless, in virtue of Christ's promises to us, the Holy Spirit will quicken the intelligence of the council or of its members. But this might be true also of any local or provincial synod.

The special guarantee that is attached to the decisions of a general council, or of the Pope when he speaks *ex cathedra,* is negative rather than positive. The charisma of infallibility means that providence will not allow an erroneous decision to be made in such circumstances. It is the business of Pope or council to use every possible human precaution, making sure that the Tradition of the Church has been fully weighed, and that the statements issued are issued in the most accurate terms available. The guarantee is simply that God would interfere sooner than allow a wrong decision.

Accordingly, we say that the Church, in defining her doctrine, is guided, not inspired. The difference between inspiration and guidance is the difference between a schoolmaster who would control the hand of a pupil while he wrote, and that of a schoolmaster who would stand by, ready to intervene if he saw him about to go wrong.

It must not be supposed, however, that this power of defining doctrines exhausts the Church's power of infallible teaching, or that doctrines can be divided into those which must be believed under pain of heresy, and those which Catholics hold merely as matters of private opinion. It is not only in her solemn conclaves, not only in the solemn definitions of her Head, that her Master's promise protects the Church from error. Just as the actions of a seditious mob may violate the security of the realm, although they do not technically constitute a riot until the Riot Act has been read, so there are theological opinions that can confidently be pronounced disloyal to Catholic teaching, even though there has not been any occasion hitherto to brand them with the stigma of heresy.

It would be manifestly false theology to deny the Assumption of our Blessed Lady, although (in spite of certain proposals made at the Vatican Council) the doctrine in question has never been defined.[11] The devotional practice

[11] Pope Pius XII defined the dogma of the Assumption of the Blessed Virgin Mary in 1950, twenty-one years after this book was written. Here and elsewhere, Knox refers to the First Vatican Council (1869-1870). — ED.

of the Church, in celebrating that event as a feast of the highest possible dignity, is sufficient guarantee that her mind is made up on the subject.

Naturally this principle cannot be pressed so as to cover every incidental phrase used in the devotional formulas sanctioned by the Church. It would be unreasonable to suppose, for example, that the Church is solemnly committed to a miraculous explanation of the phenomena that attend the exposition of St. Januarius's relics, although the second Nocturn of his feast appears to mention them among his miracles.[12] For the ordinary devout Catholic, common sense will be a sufficient guide in determining what the ordinary magisterium of the Church does and does not teach; if this fails, he may safely fall back upon the common sense of the theologians.

The Church as a teaching body is not bound to pronounce at once on each theological difficulty that occurs; sometimes she suspends her judgment, and more particularly in cases where some branch of human learning, such as history or the natural sciences, threatens to have its

[12]What is believed to be the blood of St. Januarius (d. c. 305), the Bishop of Benevento who was martyred during the Diocletian persecution, liquefies when exposed in the cathedral of Naples, where it is kept as a relic.

repercussions in theology. It is her practice, however, when she sees or suspects that the dogmatic assertion of theories hitherto unproved will confuse the minds of the simple, to regulate by her decrees the teaching that may be given on such matters by those who are her own subjects.

Thus, while the Copernican system of astronomy still rested upon very insecure foundations of argument, the Holy Office insisted that it might be taught only as a hypothesis, not as an established fact, and inflicted a sentence of nominal imprisonment upon Galileo Galilei, when he went back upon his promise to conform to the decision. As Bellarmine pointed out in writing to Foscarini, the sentence was not irreversible; if real proof of the hypothesis were forthcoming, it would be necessary to reconsider the interpretation of Scripture that had determined the action of the Holy Office.[13] This action, then, was disciplinary in its character; and the doctrinal position involved was only that which, in the opinion of the judges, was safest in view of the knowledge then available.

[13]This was the response of St. Robert Bellarmine (1542-1621), Jesuit Cardinal, teacher, writer, and Doctor, to Carmelite provincial Paolo Foscarini, who supported Galileo, claiming that Galileo's theory was not opposed to Scripture.

This principle applies in our own day to some of the answers given by the Roman congregations upon such matters as biblical criticism. The decision that a given view "cannot safely be taught" means that, in our present state of knowledge, the arguments alleged for it are not significant enough to outweigh the harm that its dissemination might involve — all this without prejudice to the possibility that fresh evidence may be forthcoming that might put the whole question on a different footing.

It might appear at first sight that the Church's teaching authority could never be compromised by excursions into the realm of natural science or of historical criticism. The proper object of infallibility is the sphere of faith and morals. But it is evident upon a little reflection that the subject is not patient of such hard-and-fast limitations. The interpretation of the Bible, in particular, is intimately bound up with the structure of theology, so largely determined by the authority of Scripture. Thus, there are some speculations of biblical criticism that might be pronounced erroneous by an infallible decree, since their acceptance would undermine the truth of the whole Christian Tradition. But where matters of less importance are concerned, it is the practice of the Church to move slowly, and to content herself with judicial pronouncements, deferring her solemn judgments until more evidence has accumulated. Such judicial pronouncements, it will easily be seen, belong by their nature to the judicial authority of the Church, which we shall consider later, rather than to her charisma of infallible teaching.

Chapter Nine

# The Church has
# legislative authority

L egislation implies initiative. We must be careful, then, not to ascribe to the Church's legislative authority certain regulations that are not of her own choosing.

It is common, for example, to hear people say that the Catholic Church forbids divorce. This is wholly inaccurate; the Catholic Church does nothing of the kind. She simply affirms, among other theological affirmations, that a duly ratified and consummated marriage cannot be dissolved by any power on earth; that, she tells us, is part of God's natural law and is further guaranteed to us by our Lord's own words.[14] Those who disagree with the Church in this matter may, if they will, call her stupid or pedantic or ill-informed; they have no right to call her harsh or tyrannical. For the prohibition comes, not from her, but from Almighty God Himself. Her action has only been that of a lawyer when we go to him to take counsel's

[14]Matt. 19:6.

opinion; he has told us what the state of the law is, but he has not made law.

In a word, such affirmations on the part of the Church really belong to the preceding chapter; they affect only her teaching office. This remains true even when she goes a step further and interprets the divine law instead of merely stating it.

Thus, there is a divine law against murder. But does this prohibition apply to the killing of an armed enemy in battle? To the killing of a man who is defending himself in a duel? To the killing of a murderer by the public executioner? To the killing of an unborn infant? All these questions are debatable, and the Church, as the guardian of a particular type of moral culture, has been forced to form her conclusions and give her answer, excusing the first and third, but not the second and fourth, from the guilt of murder. But here, once more, her part has not been that of a legislator who decides that a thing shall be so; it has been that of a teacher (an oracle, if you will) who decides that the thing is so. The prohibition of dueling and of child-murder comes, not from the Church, but from God. Our conviction that such practices are forbidden arises out of the infallibility that belongs to the Church in the sphere of morals. Our observance of the prohibition arises, not from our loyalty to the Church, but from the submissiveness of creatures to their Creator.

There is, however, a different kind of "interpretation" that does imply the active exercise of legislative power. The law of England does not forbid murder; it simply reaffirms the divine prohibition against murder. But in fulminating a death penalty against the murderer, the law of England is acting on its own initiative; otherwise it would be impossible for the sovereign to exercise his right of reprieve. Similarly, the law of England is only executing a divine commission when it sets money apart for the relief of the indigent poor. But when it decides the proportion in which the burden of poor relief is to fall on this citizen or on that, the law of England acts on its own initiative; legislation is needed.

So it is with the Catholic Church. She does not forbid suicide; she merely interprets the law of God in declaring that it is wrong. But when she goes further and denies Christian burial to the man who commits deliberate suicide, she legislates. Again, it is God's command that His creatures should worship Him. But that this worship should take the form of attending Mass every Sunday is a piece of ecclesiastical legislation. The substance of the command, in such cases, comes from God Himself; the detailed application of its fulfillment is prescribed, not by God Himself, but by the Church.

In other matters, the state forbids or prescribes things not forbidden or prescribed by the law of God, for the general good of its subjects. Thus, it forbids certain forms of gambling, although gambling is not in itself wrong; it insists that every citizen should learn to read and write, although this is not part of man's duty as a moral being. Similarly, the Church legislates for her own subjects even in matters where the law of God has left them free, for the sake of their general good. She forbids (in the West) the marriage of the clergy, although marriage is in itself a good and honorable thing. She prescribes abstinence on Fridays during Lent, although the divine law has given us no precept of abstaining. The incidence of such ecclesiastical precepts upon the ordinary layman is remarkably light; but there are instances to be found in which we have to say, "This is the law, not of God, but of His Church."

The Church, then, is not merely an assembly of witnesses, pledged to keep intact, by faithful tradition, a set of dogmatic truths and of moral principles. It is also a living corporation, with its powers vested in certain definite officials, capable of legislating in the face of emergencies. This is true of most religious bodies, as it is true of most voluntary organizations. Most of them are limited, to a certain extent, by their trust-deeds; they cannot alter their whole scope and function without committing corporate suicide, and risking the loss of whatever property they hold. But most of them have powers of legislating in detail, and binding their members by the legislation. To that extent, it is clear that there is nothing exceptional, nothing outrageous, about the claim of the Catholic Church to bind the consciences of her own subjects and to punish contumacy by expulsion.

No, what gives her action, legislative or judicial, its peculiar character is that she, almost alone among the religions, claims to be the sole means through which the human soul can achieve its supernatural end — claims, therefore, that her judgments have validity beyond the grave. Even if our Lord had not told His Apostles that whatever they bound on earth would be bound in Heaven,[15] the principle might have been inferred from the mere facts of the case. To be outlawed from your country meant, when that penalty was in vogue, death at the hands of your personal enemies. To be outlawed from Christendom means peril of spiritual death.

[15]Matt. 16:19.

It is true that the Church does not attach "censures" to her legislation except in a few cases where the gravity of the offense makes it necessary; so that the offender can be pardoned, on condition of his repentance, by any priest qualified to hear confessions. It is true that not all her regulations are binding *sub gravi*, i.e., entail the guilt of mortal sin if they are transgressed. It is true that ignorance or doubt as to the existence of the law, sometimes even mere inadvertence, excuse from guilt. But when all this is said, it remains true that an action indifferent in itself, such as eating meat on a Friday, may imperil the eternal salvation of a soul. He who transgresses any part of the law, as Scripture points out, transgresses the whole law;[16] the guilt that defiance entails is not measured by the inherent gravity of the action involved. He who neglects to hear the Church has chosen his part with the heathens and the publicans.[17]

The Church, in her official teaching, claims of her subjects an interior assent. But when the Church legislates, the attitude that she expects from her subjects is one of the will rather than one of the mind. True, there are

[16]James 2:10.
[17]Cf. Matt. 18:17.

doctrines presupposed in her legislation to which intellectual assent is necessary, e.g., the fact of the Church's legislation about the Lenten fast makes it intellectually certain that fasting in general is a sacrifice acceptable to Almighty God. But all legislation, especially where it is detailed in its matter and local in its scope, involves considerations of policy. Is it politic (to take a simple case) that such and such a country, where Protestantism is in the ascendant, should have a hierarchy of its own, or that it should remain under vicars-apostolic? Is it politic that a particular set of matrimonial regulations should be promulgated in a given country, where they will be resented by the civil power? In such matters, the authorities of the Church, whether they are local authorities or central, depend upon the exercise of human prudence; infallible in her doctrines, the Church is not inerrant in her policy.

Catholics, then, cannot rest content with believing the Church when she speaks as the mouthpiece of an infallible teacher. They must be prepared, further, to acquiesce in her decisions when they are confessedly fallible; to acquiesce in them even at the sacrifice of pocketing their private opinions. This is a matter, not of faith, but of loyalty. In many cases, the sacrifice will be considerable — when, for example, the Church's legislation runs counter to their own national or political ideals. But they are ready to make the sacrifice because they recognize that the Church must be allowed to have a voice, even in national affairs where her own ultimate well-being is affected, and that anything is better than separation from her. They are subjects of a supernatural kingdom, and, where loyalties conflict, that loyalty takes precedence over any other.

In the Church, as in the state, a local regulation has the same force and demands the same obedience as a central regulation, if it is enacted with due formalities. A national synod of bishops, or a single bishop legislating for his own diocese, can bind the faithful under pain of mortal sin, and even inflict canonical penalties, so long as the authority in question does not exceed its limited powers. For the most part, however, the competence of such local authorities does not extend beyond the definition in detail of what is already the precept of the universal Church. For example, the Church commands us to receive Communion at Easter; the local bishop decides how long a period before and after Easter Day shall be available for the satisfying of the obligation.

It is impossible that the legislation of the Church should, in its principles, run counter to the law of God.

# The Church has legislative authority

The Church could not, for example, have withdrawn the chalice from the laity in the West if she had not been assured by her own infallible tradition that Christ is received entire under either species.[18]

Ecclesiastical legislation is set, therefore, in a framework of divine jurisprudence that is fixed, immutable, and universal in its application. It is impossible for the Church in any circumstances to abrogate the law of God. She could not, for example, from whatever considerations of expediency, justify assassination or sanction bigamy. But it is possible to conceive instances in which the incidence of the divine law is conditioned by her legislation. Thus, the divine law forbids rebellion against a constituted government; but in a case of disputed succession, the Church's sanction may define whether a particular government is legitimately constituted or not. The divine law declares a duly ratified and consummated marriage indissoluble; but the conditions under which a marriage can be duly ratified may, where her own subjects are concerned,

---

[18] Although in the early Church, the faithful usually received Communion under both species, in the twelfth century it became customary to receive only under the species of bread. In recent years, Communion has once again been given under both species.

be the subject of the Church's legislation. It is at such moments of divided sympathies and of darkened counsel that Catholics will need loyalty and patience, if the clamor of misrepresentation is to leave their faith unharmed.

Chapter Ten

# The Church has judicial authority

We have already considered one kind of jurisdiction which the Catholic Church enjoys — namely, that which is exercised in the sacrament of Confession, or, as theologians say, in the internal forum. Even if the Church had no need, in her corporate capacity, of judges and of tribunals, one court would still remain: the little court of two persons that meets in the confessional. In that court, Almighty God is Himself the Prosecutor, is Himself (in the person of His priest) the Judge. The penitent is himself the defendant, himself King's Evidence of his own misdoings.

Let us suppose a layman and a missionary priest are shipwrecked on a desert island, within the limits in which the priest's faculties hold good. They may live there for years, cut off from the rest of Christendom. That spiritual court can still be set up, that sacramental jurisdiction can still be exercised, month after month, year after year. It is part of the Church's ministerial office.

But the judicial authority of the Church is not confined to the internal forum, is not bounded by the horizon of the confessional. The Church is a body corporate, with her own trust-deeds and her own laws; she must, then, enjoy judicial powers in this corporate capacity of hers, whenever doubt or dispute arises. And these, it is to be observed, are quite distinct from, and exist side by side with, the judicial powers of the state.

Heretics at various times, with a tendency that may roughly be described as Anabaptist, hold that the state, as an unsupernatural institution, has no jurisdiction over Christian men; emancipated from the bondage of the flesh, they owe obedience to none save spiritual superiors. The Catholic Church has always recognized the simultaneous existence of two streams of authority, each derived ultimately from God: secular authority, which belongs by right to the state, and ecclesiastical authority, which belongs by right to the Church. True, St. Paul does his best to dissuade Christians from going to law with one another before the heathen courts of his day; they ought rather to submit their differences to arbitration by members of their own Body.[19] But it is evident that this is only a rebuke to

[19] 1 Cor. 6:1ff.

the litigiousness of his converts, not a denial of the competence of those heathen courts to which he alludes. The powers that be, even when Nero is the world's autocrat, are ordained by God.

Ecclesiastical jurisdiction, then, is not a substitute for state action; but the Church, as a perfect and independent society, has the right, within her own sphere, to judge her subjects. Such powers are necessary even for the due exercise of her teaching authority. If a priest (such as Arius) or a bishop (such as Nestorius) is accused of heterodoxy, it is not enough, as a rule, for the Church to condemn in the abstract the teaching supposedly given. To safeguard the faith of the simple, she must further determine whether the accused person has in fact been responsible for such teaching; and, if he has, whether he is worthy to enjoy any longer the position he has abused. When the Church makes a solemn pronouncement upon some controversy that has agitated the Christian world, her infallibility may extend, not only to the merits of the doctrines in question, but to a dogmatic fact, i.e., to the statement that such and such a teacher has actually been guilty of the heresy alleged. But it is to be observed that an ordinary ecclesiastical court, in pronouncing judgment upon a heterodox teacher, does not define Christian doctrine unless the Church solemnly adopts and ratifies the decision as a doctrinal one. To this principle the Church herself bears eloquent witness, when she allows one court to reverse the proceedings of another, as happened in the rehabilitation of St. Joan of Arc.[20]

Thus the Church would be compelled, if only at intervals, to set up judicial tribunals, merely to safeguard her teaching office. But it is obvious that, apart from this, she must act as judge in controversies connected with discipline rather than with doctrine. Legislative authority implies a judicial authority corresponding to it. No code in the world can be so nicely adjusted to meet all possible emergencies that it will not sometimes call for interpretation in detail. Moreover, legislation is fruitless until judicial procedure establishes its relation to fact.

The subjects of the Church have rights one against the other in matters of purely spiritual concern. One bishop has rights against another bishop; the priest has rights of appeal against his ordinary; religious orders have their interrelations with the secular priesthood. Despite all the

[20]St. Joan of Arc (1412-1431), French heroine who led the French army against English invaders and was burned to death for alleged heresy, but later declared innocent.

appearance of uniformity that the Catholic system presents, there are a thousand opportunities of dispute. And although Catholics, and the Catholic clergy in particular, rate highly the virtue of obedience, it is inevitable that, in a worldwide Church, permanent courts should exist for the settlement of such troubles. The laity, it is true, are not often amenable to this spiritual procedure; but sometimes they, too, must have recourse to it, particularly in matrimonial causes.

Probably nothing contributes more powerfully to the impression that the Catholic Church is a soulless tyranny than the perpetual stream of rescripts and decisions that flows out of Rome in virtue of this judicial necessity. Yet it is hard to see why the Churches of the world should not find their court of arbitration at Rome, as the nations of the world find, today, their court of arbitration at Geneva.

It is the duty of a citizen to accept the award made by the supreme court of justice in his own country, even where it is given against him. Similarly, it is the duty of a Catholic, if he cannot accept the ruling of a diocesan authority, to make his appeal to Rome, not to any secular tribunal. And the judgment of Rome will be final; it would be impossible for a Catholic to appeal beyond Rome to any secular tribunal whatsoever. For the authority of the Church is a source of jurisdiction completely independent of any other; and, granted that the Church has any right to exist at all, her judicial competence could be denied only by one who was a rebel against all authority and against the common welfare of his fellowmen.

The Church employs one form of judicial process that deals with a peculiar subject matter: the process that precedes the beatification and canonization of saints. The motive force in such matters, the agitation that leads to a positive result, is always popular; it is a popular instinct that demands, rightly or wrongly, the recognition of sanctity in a given career.

The Church as an official body only provides machinery that can be set in motion; and the form this machinery takes is that of a "friendly suit." The Church briefs an ecclesiastical lawyer to contest the claim, urged by another ecclesiastical lawyer of the deceased person to the title of sanctity. If the claim is rejected, the verdict is simply not proven; we cannot conclude anything positive from the failure of the claimant to establish his case. If, however, the judgment of the court is favorable, it is followed by beatification and (after fresh judicial process) by canonization. In this latter case, the decision of the

Church is infallible; she claims here to judge infallibly on a point of fact; she can recognize heroic sanctity when she sees it.

Nor is her claim a very exacting one. Doubtless by now there are millions of souls in Heaven; doubtless many thousands of them practiced heroic virtue in an unusual degree. All the Church claims is that some few of these were so signally marked out by evidences of the divine favor that their sanctity may be presumed with absolute safety. This infallible certainty does not, however, attach to those popular canonizations that were in vogue before the modern procedure came into force.

Our Lord committed to His Church, not only powers of binding, but powers of loosing. These apply, primarily, to the sacrament of Penance. But they also extend to the jurisdiction of the Church in the external forum, since the Church has the right to dispense individuals from the obligation of her own laws.

To take a simple instance, it is a good principle on the whole that first cousins should not marry, and the Church accordingly forbids the practice. But the harm resulting would result, not from one or two infringements of the law, but from its wholesale neglect. The Church, then, does nothing preposterous when she dispenses from this law in individual cases, where good reason can be shown for it. Her power of dispensing follows from her power of legislation. She cannot in any circumstances dispense a soul from the obligations of the divine law.

Chapter Eleven

# The Church has authority
# to enforce her judgments

The Church does not claim the power of inflicting the death penalty. It is true that Popes have done so, but always within their own temporal dominions, where they exercised a temporal sovereignty; the same may be said about the prince-bishops of the Middle Ages. But whenever the death penalty has been inflicted, outside these regions, for heresy or for a moral, as opposed to a criminal, offense, it is the state code that has made itself responsible for the decree. The Church has given her verdict; the state has pronounced sentence.

On the other hand, it would not be true to say that the Church has never claimed the power of using physical, as opposed to moral, coercion. The death penalty exists merely for the protection of society; and the Church can protect her own members, as such, from the infection of heresy by excommunication. But other punishments, such as that of imprisonment, may have and are meant to have a corrective, not merely a vindictive, effect; they are ordained partly for the good of the criminal himself. The imprisonment of a house-breaker is not merely designed to give society five years' rest from his activities; it is meant also to make the house-breaker wonder whether it is worth it, to suggest to him the possibility, and the propriety, of finding other ways of living. It is unfortunately probable that the mechanization of our modern police methods has robbed this moral appeal of whatever practical worth it had. But it remains true that the ideal of the Church in inflicting any kind of physical punishment has always been the correction of the offender.

It may be observed, further, that when the discipline referred to was in vigor, the punishments inflicted by ecclesiastical authorities were usually lighter than those which secular authorities would have inflicted for a similar offense. Those who were enabled (by the legal system then in vogue) to do so were glad enough to claim "privilege of clergy" and submit themselves to an ecclesiastical tribunal rather than to a secular one.

Whatever abuses may have arisen from the system in practice, it is clear that, in theory, the Church's interference in police matters was a laudable one. It meant that, wherever possible, the authority given to the Apostles "to build up, and not to destroy" should take precedence of the rough-and-ready laws by which medieval society protected itself against the criminal.

In practice, the infliction of physical penalties by the Church is all but obsolete; and it is doubtful whether a re-Catholicized Europe would demand any restoration of the old system, now that our police organization has become simplified and centralized. Meanwhile it is certain that the Church uses methods of moral coercion. The authority to legislate would be useless, as we have seen, without the authority to judge; the authority to judge would be equally useless without the authority to enforce judgment by penalties.

It is certain that this authority was, from the earliest times, claimed as inherent in the powers of the apostolate. St. Paul, condemning a certain class of delinquents, orders his converts not even to eat with such a one. Elsewhere he tells the Corinthians to "deliver such a one to Satan for the destruction of the flesh, that the spirit may be saved in the day of our Lord Jesus Christ";[21] he speaks also of "Hymeneus and Alexander, whom I have delivered up to Satan, that they may learn not to blaspheme."[22]

[21] 1 Cor. 5:5.
[22] 1 Tim. 1:20.

# The Church on Earth

Whatever be the precise force of these expressions, it is clear that nothing less than excommunication can be meant. And the sentence clearly takes here its most solemn form. It is no mere expulsion from a voluntary association. It is exclusion from the communion of the faithful.

A religious body that does not regard itself as divinely instituted — that is, as the unique means by which man can attain his supernatural end — can afford to exclude rotten members light-heartedly enough, whether for moral delinquency or for heterodoxy. It acts as any other voluntary association would act if it became clear that its membership was being enjoyed by men who were out of harmony with its spirit and out of touch with its ambitions. But the Catholic Church, when she excommunicates, is depriving men of the normal means of sanctification that Christ has instituted. A person under the ban of excommunication loses the right to attend Mass; he may no longer receive the sacraments; nor has he any share in the indulgences and public prayers of the Church. Even with all these spiritual helps, it is not easy to save one's soul. To be cut off from them is to be in the greatest peril. The sentence of excommunication, therefore, is a terrible thing; and it is a weapon invoked, today, only against individuals who are notoriously troubling the peace of the Church or against those who are guilty of some few special forms of misdemeanor, fortunately rare.

There are, however, various minor "censures" that are more frequently inflicted. Priests who are causing public scandal, or refuse obedience to the legitimate commands of their superiors, can be punished with suspension from their clerical functions. And in order to mark her detestation of certain sins, or to emphasize the gravity of certain prohibitions, the Church occasionally "reserves" such offenses — that is, she does not allow her priests to bestow sacramental absolution on those who confess them until they are specially commissioned to do so by a bishop or (in a few cases) by the Holy See itself.

In a word, the discipline of the Church is nowadays extraordinarily mild, especially toward the laity. But this mildness does not betoken any doubt of her own authority to inflict punishments, whether temporal or spiritual. It is due only to her conviction, founded on experience, that there is more danger of breeding despair or revolt than of encouraging a lax conscience.

Chapter Twelve

# The Church's role
# differs from the state's

Ideally, the position of the Church is that of a perfect society within a Christian country, which grants it official recognition as the religion, not merely of each citizen taken individually, but of the citizens as a group. This official recognition will imply mutual relations at various points; indeed, the perfect relations between the Christian Church and the Christian state have been compared, not without justice, to the relations between the human soul and the human body.

Imagine an entirely Catholic country, which gives full freedom to the Church to perform her own rites, to build schools and to teach in them, to celebrate marriages that are *ipso facto* valid at law, to provide chaplains for the armed forces, the hospitals, the prisons, and so on — all this is not yet the Catholic ideal. For an absolutely pagan government might quite reasonably grant such concessions as this, merely on the ground that the state was bound to comply with the wishes of a strong majority among its subjects. The Church so situated is still not an established Church, and so falls short of the complete Catholic ideal.

The ideal Catholic state would not necessarily finance the Church out of public revenue, since the duty of supporting the clergy is one that falls upon the faithful individually. Nor would it necessarily give the clergy, as such, representation in the public legislature, although such provisions are natural enough where a non-elective chamber exists. But it would cooperate with the Church in achieving what is the joint aim of both the moral and spiritual welfare of the citizens.

For instance, it would shoulder the burden of public education, as most states now do, but at the same time it would make religious education an essential part of the curriculum and would leave the management of this entirely at the Church's disposal. It would enforce the decisions of the Church in matters that affect the general morality of the citizens, e.g., its marriage regulations, its provisions against immoral and blasphemous literature, and its proscription of secret societies that menace, or are liable to menace, the position of Church and state alike. The public activities of the nation — the opening of Parliament, for example, or of the Law sessions — would be

## The Church's role differs from the state's

inaugurated by official ceremonies of religion. Even the special legislation of the Church for her own subjects as such — the disciplinary regulations, for example, that affect the position of the clergy — would have the force of law; so that a priest rebelling against his ecclesiastical superiors might be amenable, not merely to ecclesiastical censures, but to punishments (if these should be deemed necessary) either carried out or recognized by the authority of the state.

On the other hand, the state would claim no control in purely religious matters; it would have no voice, for example, in the nomination of bishops, unless this right were conceded as a matter of privilege, or possibly in view of some temporal powers exercised by the bishops as officials of the state itself.

All this is an ideal, and one depending for its realization upon the goodwill of both parties; the Church would not feel justified, for example, in inviting any foreign interference to impose such a system upon an unwilling nation. It is notorious, however, that a nation or any large group, even if its members are individually Catholic or in great part Catholic, is always liable to be jealous of the Church's influence and to treat her as a rival institution. In practice, then, the relations between Church and state are a matter of adjustment, even in purely Catholic countries; and the claim for which the Church agitates is not the claim to influence the councils of a nation positively, but the claim that she ought to enjoy her own liberties undisturbed, that Catholics should suffer under no civil disabilities, that Church appointments should be subject to no civil control, that she should have the right of managing the education of Catholic children and should not be unfairly handicapped in a country that makes public grants in aid of voluntary education. All these claims seem reasonable enough from the standpoint of an ordinary Englishman; yet it is a significant fact that there are very few countries in the world where all are in practice conceded. Progressives in the name of humanity, reactionaries in the name of patriotism deny to the Church, almost everywhere, the rights enjoyed by other religious bodies.

Solicitous for the consciences of her own subjects, which may easily suffer from the problems of a dual allegiance, the Church always attempts to promote a *modus vivendi* with the secular authorities, even where she might legitimately stand on her dignity. Thus, she has at times acquiesced, although always under protest or as a matter of privilege, in arrangements that have left the appointment of bishops partly under secular control. It need hardly be added that, wherever this system has been in force, the spiritual rights of the bishops so appointed have depended entirely on their recognition by the Universal Church, not upon any recognition by the local government.

Although at times in the past there have been disputes between Church and state that concerned the relations of Church and state as such, and although sometimes rulers of the Church, acting merely as individual men, have tried to use the power of the Church for political ends, to-day the "interference" of the Church is not directly concerned with those relations.

The "interference" question arises from the fact that there are, in various parts of the world, bodies of Catholics who owe their temporal allegiance to a Protestant or a free-thinking government. It is inevitable that Catholics, in such circumstances, should invoke the advice of the clergy, their natural guides in matters of conscience, to determine their attitude in view of a political crisis. The clergy, who share the same national prejudices, are not always safe guides; there will be hotheads among them who counsel desperate measures. In that case, it is for the bishops to regulate, as well as they can in times of upheaval, the conduct of their own clergy. And finally, since the bishops, too, may well be partisans in such a controversy, they, in their turn, will sometimes feel the need of consulting a central, supranational authority that will resolve their doubts.

Any candid critic will recognize that the influence of Rome on such occasions is a moderating and a tranquillizing influence. The policy of the Holy See is always to prevent, if possible, the outbreak either of wars or of civil disturbances accompanied by violence. The Church would sooner trust to the influence of time for the settling of legitimate grievances, than risk the lives of innocent persons through the breakdown of civic order. Often enough she is criticized by her own children, in the heat of the moment, for her refusal to embitter strife and to prejudge controversies. In particular, she refrains from passing judgment upon the guilt of public acts while the evidence is still obscured by national animosities.

With regard to the Middle Ages, when papal activities often seemed merely political, it must be remembered that the polity of Europe was very different. All Western Europe was Christian and, ideally at least, united in Christian brotherhood. Of this united society the Pope was the unquestioned spiritual head — leaving out of consideration admitted heretics. The emperor claimed to be the temporal head, but his authority was never recognized outside Germany and Italy, and even those countries had usually to be asserted by force.

Yet temporal rulers in one way or another can, and could then, exercise grave influence over the souls of their subjects. Consequently, the papacy, asserting its universal authority in the interests of the salvation of its subjects, tried to prevent bad or mistaken temporal princes from using the authority that they were wielding disastrously by forbidding their Christian subjects, i.e., all their subjects, to support them in their impiety by obeying them. This naturally produced hostility from those rulers, especially from the emperors, who themselves claimed universal authority, and at times even direct divine appointment. In the heat of conflicts thus started, it is true that individual popes sometimes made excessive claims, sometimes made too great a use of spiritual weapons, and sometimes allowed themselves to become identified with the assertion of Italian independence to such an extent as to seem mere politicians. But all this does not touch the fundamental truth of the Church's claim to complete independence, and to absolute authority in the prosecution of the work of salvation of souls, for which Christ founded her.

It does, however, raise the question of whether it is ever justifiable for the Church to dispense the citizens of a

Catholic country from allegiance to the temporal government, if that government is hindering the salvation of souls. On this point, it goes without saying that, where Church and the state are true partners, the Church is recognized as being the higher institution of the two, since it is ordained to a nobler end: the eternal salvation of souls. The practical methods used in cases of conflict have varied at different times.

In the Middle Ages, when all of Western Europe, to which normally the knowledge and outlook of Churchmen were limited, was definitely Catholic, the Church was clearly able to secure her end more effectively against a hostile prince. If the rulers of the Church judged that the government of a particular man was detrimental to the eternal salvation of subjects, it was possible for her to remedy the evil, by an action that amounted to an order to those subjects to find another ruler whose power would not prejudice that which is alone of ultimate importance. Consequently, the popes claimed the right, not merely to free subjects from their allegiance, but to forbid them to continue to obey.

At the Renaissance, from various material causes, monarchy began to consolidate its position and claim absolute powers; a new doctrine then arose, that kings ruled by divine right and were responsible to nobody except Almighty God Himself. In France, this doctrine produced that strange monster, Gallicanism, with its principle of "*L'eglise, c'est moi.*" In England the sentence of deposition fulminated against Elizabeth (then nominally a Catholic) by St. Pius V,[23] coming as it did at a time of change when the majority of Englishmen were no longer obedient to the Pope, made the difficulties of Catholics considerably greater. Later, English Catholics were asked to denounce as "impious and damnable" a doctrine (that of the Church's power to depose a Christian monarch) that had been accepted without scruple in the Middle Ages, and which was still defended by the best theological opinion.

Since then, the gradual downfall of absolute monarchy throughout Europe has removed the whole question from the sphere of practical politics. It is an accepted principle in most countries that government is conditioned by the will of the governed; nor is it possible for one man or a small group of men to tyrannize over the consciences of a majority, except where power has been forcibly usurped. And where power has been forcibly usurped, the obedience of the subject is exacted by *force majeure*; he needs

[23]St. Pius V (1504-1572), Pope from 1565.

no appeal to Rome to decide for him the question of whether the adventurer has a right to rule.

In practice, then, as Pope Pius IX said in a sermon, "No one now thinks any more of the right of deposing princes, which the Holy See formerly exercised, and the Supreme Pontiff even less than anyone."[24] Some theologians have even maintained that the Deposing Power, when it was in vigor, belonged inseparably to the constitution of society at the time and had no permanent meaning. But it seems difficult to deny to the Supreme Pontiff, even under modern conditions, the right to decide whether an existing government can or cannot claim the allegiance of its subjects *de jure* as well as *de facto*. It is certain that, as Pope Boniface VII laid down in his constitution *Unam sanctam*, "If the earthly power goes astray, it will be judged by the spiritual power." It will receive the fruits of that award, if not in time, then in eternity.

[24]Quoted in *Addis and Arnold's Catholic Dictionary*, s.v. "Deposing Power."

Part Three

# The seat of authority
# in the Church

Chapter Thirteen

# The bishop has authority
# over his diocese

The normal unit of the Catholic Church is the diocese: a territorial area ruled by a bishop, who has his cathedral church in fixed spot, with its proper complement of canons, and takes from that spot (or from the area itself) his official title.

Where the Catholic body is still only a missionary body, and needs to be financed and controlled from without, instead of forming a self-dependent unit, it is sometimes governed instead by a vicar-apostolic, who enjoys an honorary title elsewhere *in partibus infidelium* — that is, in those Eastern districts where the old sees are no longer a living reality. A vicar-apostolic rules as a bishop rules in his own diocese and normally enjoys the same rights and privileges. Sometimes, however, an unconsecrated priest, with special powers, is entrusted with jurisdiction over a missionary area of this kind. In contrast with such a mere delegate, the diocesan bishop enjoys a position of relative independence.

Necessarily, this independence is only relative. A bishop claims the loyalty of the faithful in his diocese only so long as he himself is in communion with the general body of Catholic bishops throughout the world; if the local bishop (as has sometimes happened) lapses into heresy or schism, his jurisdiction ceases, and a fresh bishop is elected to the same see. Even apart from such extraordinary cases, the authority of the bishop is necessarily to some extent conditioned by its relations with the central government of the Church. Thus, a division of dioceses may take away from him part of the area which he formerly ruled. Or a union of dioceses, or redistribution of them, may cause him to vacate his title; and although on such occasions it is customary for the bishop to resign, his consent is not necessary. This was the position of certain bishops in France after the Concordat between Pius VII and Napoleon.

As we have seen, an appeal from the bishop's decision lies to the center of judicial authority in Rome. The recognition of the Holy See is always necessary to the regularity of a bishop's election. Any legislation that is enacted by a pope or a general council is binding without the sanction of the local bishop, unless it is expressly stipulated in such legislation that it is to await local promulgation.

# The bishop has authority over his diocese

Subject to these limitations, the bishop has the whole responsibility for the souls under his charge. His doctrinal teaching, indeed, is not infallible, although (when it is officially given) it should be presumed to be the teaching of the Church unless and until the contrary is known. But his legislation holds good in its own right, and his judicial sentences, censures, etc., although they can be appealed against, are binding within the area of his jurisdiction. It is his business, too, according to the earliest belief of the Church, to hand on to his successor unimpaired that Faith which he received from his predecessor; hence the "profession of Faith" which is customarily made by a bishop before his death.

Chapter Fourteen

# General councils are infallible

I ndividually, as we have seen, the bishops of the Catholic Church are witnesses to the deposit of Faith that is handed down through the centuries from one holder of the office to the next. From the earliest times, appeal was made (in case of doubt) from one local tradition to another, the antiquity of the see and the dignity of its origins being taken into account. The teaching commission that our Lord gave to His Apostles — going so far as to declare that anyone who was unfaithful to their teaching would incur damnation[25] — is compatible with the possibility that an individual bishop will err, but not with the possibility that the whole College of Bishops, the successors of the Apostles throughout the world, should fall into a common error. This latter possibility would destroy the certainty of the Christian revelation altogether. Accordingly, our Lord gave to His Apostles collectively the

[25]Cf. Matt. 10:14-15.

promise that his Holy Spirit would "guide them into all truth."[26]

Thus, in theory, an infallible decision might be obtained by circularizing all the bishops of the Catholic communion with a questionnaire and noting down the points over which their agreement was unqualified. But in practice, the decision of theological difficulties entails a more elaborate process; the exact significance of terms has to be weighed, the exact bearing of various documents to be considered, and so on. For such purposes, it is obvious that truth is best attainable by a *viva voce* discussion. The tenets, therefore, that are accepted as part of the Christian Tradition on the strength of the infallibility resident in the episcopal college are those tenets which have been defined in the twenty general councils that have so far been held in Christendom.[27]

These general or ecumenical councils have to be distinguished, not only from various local councils, which never claimed infallibility for their own decisions, but also from certain assemblies that, although formally representative

[26]Cf. John 16:13.

[27]The Second Vatican Council (1962-1965) brings the total to twenty-one. — ED.

of the whole Church, have never in fact been accepted by it. What, then, is the criterion by which we are to decide between a true and a false "general council"? The countenance lent by secular authorities, which was once held by Protestants to be of vital importance (thus *The Thirty-Nine Articles* maintain, "General councils may not be gathered together without the commandment and will of princes"), is not likely to be appealed to nowadays; we no longer live under the Tudors. Modern Protestants are more apt to take the point of view that, "However large be the number of bishops present, no guarantee is thereby afforded that they faithfully represent the mind of the Universal Church. That which alone can show this is the after-reception of the decisions of the council by the different parts of the Church."[28]

The preposterousness of such a challenge is easily demonstrated. The sentiment expressed is clearly meant to hold good even if every single Catholic bishop in the world attends the council. The after-reception of their decisions by the various parts of the Church does not mean, then, their after-reception by the various bishops, since this would attach more importance to the bishops taken

[28]Bishop Gibson, *The Thirty-Nine Articles*, p. 536.

individually than to the bishops taken collectively. It must refer to the after-reception of the decision by the faithful at large. And this clearly means that, so far from having to teach the clergy and the laity, the bishops must go to the clergy and the laity to know whether their own decisions are infallible or not!

Further, it may well be questioned whether, on this principle, there ever has been a general council in Christendom. For the decisions made by the Council of Ephesus in 431, the third of the series, still remain unaccepted by the Nestorians after fifteen centuries. Are the Nestorians "part of the Church"? If so, the Council of Ephesus has no authority. If not, why not? Because they were condemned by the Council of Ephesus? But at that time, they were part of the Church, and they never accepted the council; therefore, the council had no ecumenical authority to exclude them!

It need hardly be pointed out that the general body of the faithful does not claim, and never has claimed, any infallible teaching authority for itself; it follows the guidance of its ecclesiastical superiors. Why is it, then, that the collection of people whom we call "the faithful" (not including the Nestorians) has in fact accepted the Ephesine decisions?

There remains only one criterion (short of sheer private judgment) by which the ecumenicity of a council can be decided. Those councils are ecumenical which the Apostolic See of Rome recognizes as such. If the Pope had no other function in the economy of Christendom, one at least must be conceded to him, unless the whole fabric of Christian theology is to be subject to perpetual alteration and revision. He must be the umpire who decides whether a council shall be accepted as a general council or not. This is, in fact, the only key to the reading of early Church history that accounts for its development; it was certainly not the imperial power that safeguarded the unalterable deposit. On the contrary, it is the secular power, from the days of Constantine's successors to the days of Queen Elizabeth, that has always been disruptive of Christian unity by slighting, in the Holy See, its only possible center of cohesion.

That is not a general council which is summoned without the direct cooperation of the Holy See. While Europe was a Christian state, it was natural that the emperor should be the actual convener of a worldwide gathering, since it rested with him to afford the necessary traveling facilities. In medieval Europe, the cooperation of secular princes, and of the emperor in particular, was needed to ensure that the gathering might be of a fully representative character. Even in the nineteenth century, the Tsar of Russia forbade the Catholic bishops resident in his dominions to attend the Council of the Vatican. But the function of the state on such occasions, properly considered, is only to remove the material obstacles that might hinder the bishops from coming together. It is the permission, at least, of the Holy See that makes the acts of a council valid from their inception.

That is not a general council which fails to obtain for its decisions the subsequent ratification of the Holy See. Indeed, in some instances, the Holy See has ratified certain decisions of a council and rejected the others. Thus the Council of Constance claims ecumenicity only for its later sessions, and the recognition given to the Council of Florence does not extend to its earlier deliberations at Basle, except for three decrees passed there. It may be objected that this power of ratification undoes the whole utility of general councils, since their authority in the last resort depends upon the authority of the Pope. It would be as reasonable to object that the whole notion of ecclesiastical infallibility undermines the position of Scripture, since the authority of the Scriptures is itself guaranteed to us by the authority of the Church. Infallibility is, after all, a negative concept, and the positive activities of a general council in collecting opinions from the whole of the Christian world, in discussing them, in elucidating terms, in drawing up formulas, and in rejecting theological over-statements is not so much time wasted merely because the authority of its proceedings rests upon recognition from outside. The Royal Assent is necessary for the passing of any bill brought forward in England, yet the Houses of Parliament are true legislative assemblies.

In a word, although our assurance that the decrees of a given council are infallible comes from the Holy See, the infallibility itself arises from the fact that the bishops of the world (the Bishop of Rome included) have deliberated, and have been prevented by the Holy Spirit from coming to any false decision. It is not necessary that all the bishops of the world should be present, or that all those present should agree to the decisions of the council at the time (although they must accept them afterward, on pain of dissenting from the voice of the Universal Church). But a council merely local in its representation, e.g., those held by the American bishops in Baltimore, has no ecumenical authority attached to its decisions; and if they should obtain such authority, this can be only through the infallibility of the Pope who ratifies them, not from any infallibility resident in the Fathers of the council themselves.

In the imaginary situation of a disagreement arising between the Pope and a majority of the bishops then in communion with the Holy See, the authority of the Pope would have to be preferred, although it is generally held that, in view of the divine promises, such a situation could not in fact arise, so long as both parties were giving their voices deliberately, without external constraint.

The disciplinary regulations made by a general council are not irreformable, but demand the same loyalty that is due to the disciplinary regulations of the Holy See.

Chapter Fifteen

# The Pope has authority over the entire Church

The Church of Rome consists of rather more than five hundred thousand persons, residing in and around the capital of Italy. It is a diocese, with a bishop of its own. According to a very ancient custom, this bishop is elected by the parish priests of some of the principal churches in the city; these are largely non-resident foreigners, including the Englishman who is also Archbishop of Westminster. The Roman Bishop, like all other bishops of the Catholic Church, has the duty of transmitting to his successors unimpaired the Faith delivered to him by his predecessors. Other churches, represented by their bishops, may err in matters of the Faith; the Church of Constantinople, as represented by its bishop Nestorius, erred; so did the Church of Canterbury, as represented by its bishop, Thomas Cranmer. The Church of Rome cannot err in matters of the Faith; for this reason, she is called the Mother and Mistress of all the other churches — that of Milan, that of Westminster, that of Chicago, and so on.

# The Church on Earth

There is, therefore, a second principle of infallibility in the Catholic Church. Its bishops sitting in council cannot err as a body; and this one bishop, the successor of Peter, Linus, and Clement, cannot err in declaring the Faith handed down to him by his predecessors, however much or little he may have consulted his fellow-bishops before making such a declaration. The charisma so granted to him is a negative one. It is possible for the Roman Pontiff, through lack of information, or even through lack of pastoral zeal, to allow errors to go for a time unchecked. But if and when he does speak as the official expounder of the Roman Tradition, the Pope is protected from error no less surely than the whole College of Bishops when they speak as the official expounders of their common Tradition.

We have seen that, but for the existence of some such single voice, it would be impossible to know where the true Church was, after so many disastrous schisms. This consideration by itself disposes of the Gallican notion that the Pope is infallible only when he acts in concert with an ecumenical council. For the council, as we have seen, is not ecumenical unless the Pope declares it to be so; and in making this declaration, it is impossible, clearly, that the council itself should have any share. In the last resort, then, infallibility lies in the Pope, not in the council; and it would be absurdly arbitrary to limit such infallibility to one particular function. It is not so that the Church interprets our Lord's appointment of St. Peter as the Rock, the Door-keeper, and the Shepherd. To appeal from the Pope to a council is to appeal from the Pope to the Pope.

Inconsistent at all times, the Gallican theory of Church authority was finally exploded by "the logic of facts." The Council of the Vatican, duly convoked from all parts of the Catholic world, discussed the very question at issue and laid it down that the Pope's solemn pronouncements were irreformable of themselves, and not through the consent of the Church. Thenceforward, Gallicanism has been self-undermined; you cannot believe in the infallibility of general councils without believing, by inference, that the infallibility of the Pope is independent of them.

The conditions of an infallible utterance are well known: the Pope should be acting in his capacity as pastor and teacher of all Christians, and he should be defining a doctrine concerning Faith or morals that is to be held by the whole Church. Where the subject matter is sufficiently important to make clearness on the point essential, the popes themselves have left their intention of making an irreformable definition absolutely beyond doubt, e.g., in the formula that concludes the decree on the Immaculate Conception.

The Roman Pontiff is not only the teacher of all Christians; he is also their ruler in spiritual matters. It would have been, humanly speaking, inevitable, even if definite charter had been given to the Church to determine her constitution, that her government should have become progressively centralized to meet her own administrative needs. We know, from the commission given by our Lord to St. Peter to feed His flock,[29] that the monarchical constitution of the Church was determined from the first in the mind of her divine Founder.

Accordingly, we regard the gradual extension of the Roman influence to the remotest parts of the Church, not as the tacit assumption of fresh powers, but as the fuller exercise of powers already held. It is inevitable that, where an institution is in its infancy and facilities of communication are lacking, much should be left to the individual initiative of "the man on the spot." The papacy, first hidden away in the catacombs, then crippled by its rivalry with the imperial power, then left at the mercy of the barbarian invasions, then hampered by the perpetual

[29]John 21:15-17.

# The Pope has authority over the entire Church

wars of medieval Europe, could only gradually assert its divinely guaranteed position as an effective law-giver and judge. But from the first, with whatever hesitations and reluctances, it is the Roman discipline that wins in the struggle; Rome could forbid the rebaptism of heretics against the protests of a Cyprian and assert her own ruling about the Paschal celebration against the venerable customs of the East. From the first, the imperial instinct is there.

Men's minds are strangely retentive of local custom, and the abuse of yesterday easily passes into an immemorial tradition. The fissiparous history of Protestantism gives abundant warning of the dangers to which the unity of the Church would have been exposed if she had not possessed, by divine appointment, a single center of effective legislation. Only twenty ecumenical councils have been held, and today the summoning of such councils is as difficult from the material point of view as it has been in any period of Christianity. It is difficult to see what influence, save that of Rome, could have restrained an infinite variety of local evagations. True, the centralization of the Church has meant uniformity; but uniformity is the seal of unity, as drill is of discipline. And there is, perhaps, no legislation in the world that is so patient of antiquarian anomalies, so tender toward vested rights, as the code of the Catholic Church.

Meanwhile, whatever irritation may be felt, here and there, among restless spirits, over the complicated procedure and inelastic methods of those "congregations" and "tribunals" which administer the business of the Church, her monarchical organization has the effect of concentrating all our loyalties upon the personality of a living individual, the representative to us at once of those united millions whose destinies he governs, and of the Master in whose name he governs them. There are temperaments, there are nationalities that are ready to devote their lives in the service of an ideal or an abstraction; but the generality of men will always find it easier to wear the badge of a representative public personage than to content themselves with personifications and symbols. This is the abiding justification of our hereditary monarchies; this is the strength and the weakness of our modem dictatorships.

The Catholic, in his inner life, is fortified by the consciousness of a loyalty higher than all human loyalties: his devotion to the Person of our Lord Jesus Christ. But he is further privileged in this: that in his public capacity, as the citizen here and now of a visible city of God, he can focus all his capacity for loyalty upon a living personality, with

# The Pope has authority over the entire Church

whose lineaments he is familiar, for whose blessing, perhaps, he has knelt. He can feel one with the millions of his alien fellow Catholics, one with the Church of Nicaea and of the catacombs, when he identifies himself with the artless cry of the Roman populace: *Viva il Papa Re!*

Biographical Note

# Ronald Knox

(1888-1957)

The Catholic Church is blessed to have among the defenders of her Faith a man of whom Evelyn Waugh said, "I can think of no man of this century who enjoyed . . . such mastery of the English language in all its varieties." Indeed, Ronald Knox, numbered among the great Catholic writers of the twentieth century, along with Hilaire Belloc, G. K. Chesterton, Frank Sheed, and Christopher Dawson, has left the Church a rich treasury of wisdom that is as elucidating and powerful in our day as it was in his.

Ronald Knox was born into a well-to-do family in 1888. His father became the Anglican Bishop of Manchester, England, but Knox was attracted to the Catholic Church at an early age. While attending Eton, a school originally dedicated to the Blessed Virgin Mary, Knox began to develop a lifelong devotion to Mary and a taste for Catholicism. Although shy, he was popular and academically brilliant.

He attended Oxford University in 1906, where he became involved in Anglo-Catholicism and felt called to the priesthood. Although aware of the doctrinal problems of Anglicanism and much influenced by G. K. Chesterton's *Orthodoxy*, he was ordained by the Church of England in 1912 and became chaplain of Trinity College in Oxford. But in 1917, after much study, unable to prove the Anglican Church's claims to catholicity, he converted to the Catholic Faith and was ordained a Catholic priest two years later.

While Catholic chaplain at Oxford University, Knox became noted for his preaching and writing. He had a talent for explaining complicated topics compellingly and with clarity and wit. With humor and well-reasoned arguments, he ridiculed the secularism, agnosticism, atheism, and the watered-down Christianity of his day.

As a popular spiritual director, Knox wrote books about retreats and about the spiritual life, and, like his contemporaries Chesterton and Dorothy Sayers, he wrote murder mysteries. Seeing in a fresh emphasis on the Bible a remedy to the decline in Christianity in his day, Knox worked for nine years on a new translation of the Bible to make the Scriptures more accessible to ordinary people. He also wrote a three-volume commentary on the New Testament.

Knox died of cancer in 1957. His clear defense of the Faith, his deep devotion to the Blessed Mother, his practical wisdom on the spiritual life, and his sermons, collected and published, live on to enrich generations of Catholics and to guide them, not only in living their Faith, but in leading others to see the fullness of truth it contains.

# Sophia Institute Press®

Sophia Institute® is a nonprofit institution that seeks to restore man's knowledge of eternal truth, including man's knowledge of his own nature, his relation to other persons, and his relation to God. Sophia Institute Press® serves this end in numerous ways: it publishes translations of foreign works; it brings out-of-print books back into print; and it publishes important new books that fulfill the ideals of Sophia Institute®. These books afford readers a rich source of the enduring wisdom of mankind. Sophia Institute Press® makes these high-quality books available to the public by using advanced technology and by soliciting donations to subsidize its publishing costs. Your generosity can help Sophia Institute Press® to provide the public with editions of works containing the enduring wisdom of the ages. Please send your tax-deductible contribution to the address below.

*For your free catalog, call:*
**Toll-free: 1-800-888-9344**

Sophia Institute Press®
Box 5284, Manchester, NH 03108
www.sophiainstitute.com

Sophia Institute® is a tax-exempt institution as defined by the Internal Revenue Code, Section 501(c)(3). Tax I.D. 22-2548708.